MW01713554

# #LivingOutLoud
# The new LOL

Karyn Stuart

#LivingOutLoud The new LOL

Published by Beautiful River Publishing



Front Cover Design by JD&J Book Cover Design
Back Cover Photo by Grumpy Panda Photography
Editing: Firstediting.com
Formatting: Polgarus Studio

For information about special discounts available for bulk purchases or for reproduction permission, contact Beautiful River Publishing at beautifulriver@att.net.



ISBN 978-0-9973521-0-8 (Kindle)
ISBN 978-0-9973521-1-5 (ePub)
ISBN 978-0-9973521-2-2 (print)

www.karynstuart.com

# Acknowledgements

To Marlene who unwittingly gave me the title for this book. A stroke of genius indeed.

To Kate, it's amazing what 80 degrees and a little inspiration can do! I know I had to stand in the ring, but the corner man makes all the difference.

To Rev. Barry Miller, this book was born that Sunday, that summer, after that question, and the rest...is history.

# Contents

# #LivingOutLoud
# The *new* LOL

So who goes to their high school reunion and ends up having such a life-changing experience they end up writing a book three weeks later? That would be me. To be honest, it was not just the reunion itself, but the stream of events that followed in this short period of time, mixed with what God was already saying and doing in my life, that brought me so rapidly to this point. So here's what happened.

I had heard sometime in the past year that my peers were planning to host a 30th class reunion, which was the first and only we had ever had since graduation. When I heard about it, I immediately, quietly, and confidently decided, *oh, I won't be doing that!*

As the time drew near and people began questioning whether or not I was going to attend, I relayed my thoughts and my decision. I had absolutely no interest in going. It wasn't that I did not care at all about any of the people I grew up with. I did wish them well and hoped they were happy and living their best lives. But I felt like everyone who was supposed to be a part of my life from that season of my life . . . already was. I may not talk to them all the time or hang out with them like we did when we were younger, but I had their phone numbers, they had mine, and we texted from time to time; birthdays, holidays, and the occasional celebrations about this or that in life.

That was all fine with me. It was all quite enough. I have never been a fan of forcing relationships to develop. I have always believed that true relationships are revealed and discovered organically, like cream that rises to the top of a bottle of raw milk. You share space and time with people in certain places and at different seasons of your life. For reasons that can only be divine, some just rise up, take on different characteristics, become more valuable to you, and they are the ones who remain. If there were people whom I grew up with that were no longer a part of my life—which did not mean that they were not important—they just were not a part of my current life. And that is okay. We have all heard that saying: some people come into your life for a season, some come for a reason, and some come forever. I believe that.

In spite of my rather firm decision, two of my friends decided to employ the full court press. It was quite clear that if I did not relent, I was going to have two persistent women riding me, guilting me, and employing any necessary tactics to get me to go. Since at my core I do not like to be stressed-out or overwhelmed, I just gave in and decided to go. And that was that.

Even after I agreed and gave my word that I would do it, I was absolutely dreading it. Despite the outward illusion of my presence, I am actually very introverted, socially awkward, and even a little shy. My life has required me to learn and employ certain socially acceptable interaction skills, but no matter where I am or what I am doing, I am usually suffering on the inside and secretly wishing I could run for the nearest door. Don't get me wrong, I absolutely love people and meeting them and getting to know them, but I am a one-on-one kind of girl. Anything that involves a group, crowd, or anything that requires me to stand out can be absolutely painful for me. Remember that, because it will contribute to an important theme throughout this book.

So I was talking to God about it and He said, "Just go, you will be pleasantly surprised."

My answer? "Yeah . . . okay."

# The Question

After I went online and got my ticket, then came the question. I get an e-mail from the reunion organizer that says something like this: "Karyn, I am looking forward to seeing you; let me know if you would like to speak during the event."

I knew in my heart I was going to be asked this question. How could I squeeze out of this without sounding like an absolute jerk? I carefully thought about the question; let me know if ***you would like to speak***. I could just directly answer that question and perhaps shut down the whole thing. Remember the earlier paragraph—anything that requires me to stand out, be out in front, or noticeable in any crowd is just not something I ever want to do.

After a few days filled with much thought and angst, I responded to her e-mail with something like this: "Regarding me speaking at the event, my preference is always to hang back and observe rather than participate. But if you wish for me to contribute I am more than happy to do so."

That was only half-true. I decided that if she came back with a counteroffer I would not drag this out, but I really was not happy about doing it at all. The response was crafted not just to address her question, but also to address a promise I'd recently made to God.

# The Promise

I was recently taking some time to evaluate my life and in particular, thinking about the many "false starts" I seem to have had over the years. While not in any way unhappy with my life in general, I felt like there were times when I was really surging ahead, powering forward, and then all of a sudden things just came to a full stop. As I looked back, I realized that this pattern had repeated itself over and over again in my life. Each time I would begin to gain some momentum toward reaching the visions and pictures of what I believe my life was designed to be, something would happen—usually my own sin—and the whole surge and force and power moving me forward would just bring me to a full and abrupt stop.

While I was thinking and praying about this, God told me, "You are right. Every time I have picked you up and placed you on the path of your future and destined course, you have hit a brick wall and come to a full stop." But I realized the train never stopped moving, it was always me who jumped off.

I envision my journey like me riding on the top of a speeding train, *Mission Impossible* style. I'm not driving or guiding the train, I'm just riding on top of it. Every now and then, a big ol' tree limb stretches across the path in front of me and knocks me flat on my back. Sometimes it's not a tree limb but a bridge overpass. It doesn't just knock me down, it knocks me out. These obstructions are weights and sins—things that so easily beset me.

It was not until I looked back that I realized that each and every time God began moving me forward in this life—in my destiny and purpose—one of those limb-like tentacles would appear with the goal of taking me out. Interestingly enough, each of those times when I fell down, I never fell off the train and the train kept moving. But each and every time I fell down, I jumped off. I plummeted to a full, abrupt, and at times violent stop. I jumped off because I felt like I was wounded and broken and damaged and not fit for the journey.

But God never required me to get off the train. What he intended was for me to bring my wounded, broken, and damaged self to Him, let Him heal me of my wounds, let Him free me of those tentacles and vines that kept pulling me back into sin, all while staying on the train and moving forward in my purpose.

So I made a promise. Good, bad, or indifferent, I would not jump off the train ever again. And for me that means I will walk through every door He opens whether I understand the purpose or not, and begin to practice a life of radical obedience.

# Back to the Story

By telling her I was happy to say a few words if that was her request, what I was really saying was, "God, if she comes back and actually asks me to do this, I will know that this is something you want me to do and I will comply." And even as I wrote those words, I knew it was going to be something I was going to do.

After a few weeks, I got another e-mail sharing the draft of the program they'd created, and she asked me specifically to share some reflections or anything else I wanted to share. Reflections? How in the world was I supposed to share some reflections when I could barely remember anything from high school at all? I was immediately stressed-out. I had no idea what I was going to say or do.

I decided not to think about it too hard because I knew that I could think that one thought to total confusion, so I basically just ignored it. I agreed to do it, and I figured that when the time came I would stand up and I would have something to share. All the way up to the time to go I was hoping that some emergency or crisis would arise so that I would have an excuse not to attend. I was ready to skip out and just breathe a sigh of relief and not have to deal with such an uncomfortable experience, even though I had paid for my ticket. But no such thing occurred.

# Do they know you are going to preach?

I was talking to my cousin before it was time to go and I told her I was going to speak. She said, "I don't understand. I thought you were going to your high school reunion. Is there going to be preaching at the reunion?"

I said, "No, there is not going to be any preaching. This is a reunion. They have a little program or something and they asked me to say a few words."

"Yeah, but do they know you're going to preach?" she asked.

"I'm not preaching; don't be ridiculous. Again, they are having a program—you know, with a couple different things they want to do—and they asked me to give some reflections. I'm not going to there to preach."

She said, "Yeah, but every time you talk, you preach. Do they know who you are?"

"That's just ridiculous, and you are ridiculous, and I'm not going to discuss this with you," I answered.

She said, "Oh, I wish I could go! I wish I could see it. This is going to be so good."

# The Reunion

So we got there and we were late—not fashionably late, just late. In fact, when we arrived, the whole group had just assembled outside so they could take the group photo, and we were the last two people, running down the ramp, trying to get in the picture. How's that for a quiet, graceful, unnoticed entrance? But amazingly and quite to my surprise, I was greeted by a beautiful and intelligent and exciting group of people and I was thrilled to see them. Everybody looked absolutely amazing. Everybody was so kind and so warm and so welcoming. In that initial moment, I was actually glad that I had come.

We took the photograph, gave our greetings, everybody hugged everybody, asked how are you and all that, and then we went inside. Shortly thereafter, the program began. When we got to the part of the program where people were going to share reflections, I had asked if I could go last, hoping I could gain some inspiration from something I heard somebody else say. But by the time it was my turn I was in the same place that I was when I'd arrived—I had nothing. So when I got up I just decided to do what I do, which is to be completely honest, and I said something like this:

> I know that I was asked to share reflections from our time in school, but the fact of the matter is, I really can hardly remember a thing. I don't know about you, but I smoked a lot of weed down through the years. I don't care what

> anybody tells you, it really does impact your memory. So, I just can't remember a whole lot of anything that went on while we were in school together. What does come to mind when I think back on those times is that line from *A Tale of Two Cities*: "It was the best of times, it was the worst of times . . ."

I was thinking about my own personal life during that season. And in that moment I became aware of the fact that, though I was standing in front of a group of people I had once known, I really had no idea what their lives were like then, and no idea who they were today. I did not know if they were happy or not happy. I did not know if they were content with the lives they lived. I did not know if they had experienced any joy, any tragedies, or any success. I had absolutely no insight at all about who they were.

It would've been easy for me to make up something to talk about from our time in high school, or tell some kind of bad joke, but in that moment I realized that the best thing I could do was not speak about the past or even speak to their present, but I could speak to our future. So that's what I did. I decided to encourage them. I decided to remind them that it was not too late for us to fulfill our dreams and goals. I just spoke some encouraging words to them. I blessed them and spoke life to them. That was it. The rest of the program went on and I had a good time. I talked to a lot of people and there was not one objectionable experience that occurred the entire night. That was amazing.

# Are you preaching tomorrow?

Among my friends who were in attendance was one of my classmates who is an attorney, who also pastors a Church with her husband not far from where we grew up. I've been to their Church a couple of times to visit and show my support, but I'm not sure if either one of them ever actually knew that I was a preacher. I'm not sure either one of them ever knew that even back when we were in high school I was preaching.

As the evening moved on and I was milling about, I went to their table to sit and chat. Her husband, Barry, said to me, "You're preaching tomorrow morning, right?"

I was thinking, *did he really just say what I thought he said?* I said, "What? I mean, I don't even have any church clothes, man; I'm totally ***not*** ready. This is all I have." I gestured toward the outfit I was wearing. "I was planning on going home in the morning."

He said, "I'm going to take that as a yes. And I mean, what you have on is fine, or if you just want to wear a robe, I've got robes. I mean, you can wear one if you want to but you can come as you are. You need to come tomorrow, I'm telling you." And I instantly knew, *okay, God, here we go. I'm going to walk through this open door.*

I didn't have any church clothes. I didn't have a Bible. I certainly did not have a message or a word prepared. I was at the class reunion, which meant I wasn't even going to get back to my friend's house before midnight. And Church started the next morning at ten. So, it was clear that if a word was going to be spoken, God was going to have to make it happen.

I think the first thing I did after I said yes was I went to one of my friends to get some support. I said, "Okay, Barry just asked me to come to his Church and preach in the morning and you have to come." I piled it on thick and said, "I came here for you, so you have to go there for me."

The evening wound down and we headed home. Before I even got back to my friend's house I kind of knew what the word was. When I got there, I read a little and prayed a little, and then I went to sleep.

# Sunday Morning

Usually these days when I have to preach, it doesn't matter how much I pray or read the Bible or talk to God, I will usually get one Scripture or one word or one phrase in my mind. And that's it. It's a miracle if I ever get a title to a message because that just rarely if ever happens. Usually it seems that I just get up and start talking and God takes it from there. It doesn't often look like what other people do when they preach. I have just decided to go with it and let God do whatever he's going to do.

This time was really not any different. I knew what the Scripture was and I had read it and actually preached it before. But I wasn't certain at all where this was going to go. I thought I would preach some version or iteration of the same message that I had preached before. But when I stood up, something different occurred. Before I even got to the message, I needed to give a bit of personal background and the epiphany that occurred leading to this Living Out Loud.

# A little history

I only spoke for a few minutes at the reunion. It was an admission that I would be looking at nametags all night because I couldn't even remember anyone's name. And it was a word of encouragement to a group of people I had not seen in at least 30 years. That was the whole of my speaking at my class reunion. Yet at the end of that short speech there were several people who came to me and said, "Wow, that was really great." One or two said, "You sound like some kind of a minister. Are you?" And then I realized that at the same time that I was in school with all of those people in that room I was also living a whole separate life, having been licensed to preach at 15 years old. Almost none of them knew that I'd spent almost every weekend of my last two years in high school not just in Church, but preaching at somebody's Church somewhere. It was an entire reality that I had managed to keep completely secret from those around me. I couldn't help thinking about that as I was preparing to preach.

The Scripture and the story were familiar to me; actually one of my favorites, John chapter 9, which tells the story of the man who was born blind. There are so many reasons why I love that story and I've actually taught it one or two times before. But as I stood up to speak this Sunday morning I realized that God was teaching me an entirely different message and I needed listen through the text. One thing many people don't realize is that when someone gets up to speak or preach a word, the first one who actually hears the message is the one who is to speak it.

I was thinking through the text and I was thinking through my life, and I realized that I had lived such a secret life that I had moved about in the midst of people who never even knew who I was; just like my cousin had mentioned earlier. This in itself was not really news to me. In recent weeks and months God had been speaking to me again and again about being honest about who I was. I had developed a consistent and well-crafted pattern of deflecting attention and denying my calling and to some degree, not even acknowledging that I was a Christian at all.

The Lord and I had many conversations about what it actually meant when I denied or hid the fact that I was in ministry. I had a well-rehearsed answer for why I did what I did. I didn't really consider myself being dishonest when I gave people my standard answers. When people would ask me anything about being in ministry, even when I was in Church and somebody would say, "Oh, that was a great word," or, "We love to hear you preach," or, "You're such a great teacher," I would say, "Oh no, I just made that whole thing up," or, "Really, I just listen to what other people say and repeat it," or, "It's a miracle! If I have come up with something that made sense we know that had to be God!" I had 100 answers memorized that I would use to devalue, depreciate, or even completely deny that I was in fact who I was.

And who I am is someone who has been called by God to not only speak his word but to demonstrate his love and his power in the earth.

I decided after many years of observation that whenever I mentioned that I was in ministry, people's attitudes and behaviors began to change. Instead of being real and honest and transparent about who they were, they began to be people who showed me a fake image of who they wanted me to see. They sent their representative instead of their real selves. They showed me the person they thought they should be; the person who was anything other than who they were.

Just mention that you are a preacher and people start talking about how they used to go to Church, how they know they shouldn't cuss as much as they do, how they believe in God but they still like to have a good time. They immediately start giving you a litany of their sins and the things they do that they know are not right. Sometimes they become defensive, confrontational, or argumentative, all because they know who you are.

It becomes very difficult for you to really get to know people; I mean *really* get to know them for who they truly are, because there's something about people knowing that you are in ministry that automatically elicits a different type of behavior. Even the Christians and quasi-pseudo-Christians then begin to change. Every time they talk to you they want to quote the Bible. They want to say some catchy little Church phrase. When you ask them how they're doing they can't just say fine anymore. Now when you say, "Hey, how are you?" they've got to say, "Praise the Lord I'm blessed and highly favored!" Or, "God is good!" or whatever the latest catchphrase of their Church or their ministry is for that hour. As soon as you get that kind of response you know how the conversation is about to go. Because even with the Christians, from that point on you know that everything that follows is going to be something fake and phony and not real.

What's the deal with that? There is nothing in me, Christian or not, that wants to spend my time with people who don't want to do anything else with me but sing hymns and discuss Scripture until they wear me out. Sometimes I just want to hang out. Sometimes I just want to go to the movies. Sometimes I just want to go to a game. For whatever reason, as soon as people find out that you are in ministry they act like you're not just a regular human being like they are.

Now, to some extent, I do understand. I guess it's a safe thing to say that ministers and pastors have been generally set apart, lifted up, and considered to be something different and even something better than everyone in the general population of people, including other Christians. We seem to receive greater honor, greater preference, and greater respect from people than everyone else. But there is this truth that even though a few of us may have been called to a preaching ministry, a five-fold ministry, or operate in one of the coveted and desirable "vocal gifts," every single person who gives their life to Jesus Christ is actually called to ministry. In 2 Corinthians 5:17-20, Paul says this:

> "*Therefore, if anyone is in Christ, he is a new creation; old things have passed away; behold, all things have become new. Now all things are of God, who has reconciled us to Himself through Jesus Christ, and has given us the ministry of reconciliation, that is, that God was in Christ reconciling the world to Himself, not imputing their trespasses to them, and has committed to us the word of reconciliation. Now then, we are ambassadors for Christ, as though God were pleading through us: we implore you on Christ's behalf, be reconciled to God.*"

I believe this Scripture speaks to all of us. We are all called to the ministry of reconciliation. So while there may be a very strong argument for why pastors, preachers, and ministers are treated differently from everybody else in the Christian world, I prefer to be treated like everybody else. I see myself in the light of my reality, where there is no reason to act different, be different, or think that I am all that much different from anyone else.

Such carefully honed answers that I had practiced over and over again for years. I told the Lord that I wasn't really lying about who I was, I just wanted people to be real about who ***they were*** around me. I'd like to meet people and know people for who they really are, and I like to know who I'm dealing with and what I'm dealing with.

In my view, the only way I could do that was if they did not know that I was a preacher. I had convinced myself that it was better that way; that I could finally find a way to meld myself into my environment and never have to stand out. I had convinced myself that in the very moment anyone knew that I didn't just go to Church but I was a leader in the Lord's Church, then that would be the end of a normal relationship. Not to mention, even in the Church there seems to be so much competition about what your gift is and what your title is. Even in a place where we're all supposed to be focused on the same goal, something as silly as a title can bring more division, more animosity, and more strife than anything you could ever imagine.

So I just decided it was easier to act like I didn't know what was going on—to act like I was not spiritual at all and just blend in with the crowd of mediocrity that was all around. That was my explanation, at least, and God really didn't go into any argument with me about any of it. The only thing He did say was, "You do know you are being dishonest and you are not speaking the truth, right?" And even after I had acknowledged to God that I had become a very consistent liar about this area of my life, I still found it very difficult to change. I had communicated that way for so long. I'd convinced myself that this was the only way I could have peace and have real relationships with other people who were normal and not weird, and this was the only way I could make my enemies stay calm and behave; if I gave them the impression that they had no reason to fear anything and nothing to feel threatened about. I was just any other person sucking up air and not making a difference.

I did not just do this about my life in Christ. I did this in every area of my life. This self-deprecation had become the disarming weapon I used to control my environment. Rather than get people worked up and obsessed with their own striving and ambition I would say things to them like, "I'm an idiot. It's a miracle I can even function in the world. If I actually did something right or got something right; it's miracle—it was probably a mistake." I always said that everyone in the room was smarter than me, more talented than me, more gifted than me.

When I did this, it seemed to eliminate the need for others to strive with me and compete with me and generally give me grief and stress. I had been doing this for so long that the words flew out of my mouth without thought, and at times without provocation. Since I made it clear upfront that there was very little value that I had to contribute, there was no expectation for me to do anything other than that. I could sit back and observe everything that was going on, and every now and then say or do something that offered value, then go right back into hiding.

I loved this kind of life. It had become peaceful and an ark of safety for me to strategically fly under the radar concerning all things. As far as I was concerned, this method had worked quite effectively for me over the years—until recently, when God seemed to have a problem with it. In order for me to hold that position, I had to ignore and depreciate and negate everything that He had done in my life. Therein lies the rub. And I learned something else about myself. There was another secret benefit to flying under the radar. That meant I always reserved the freedom and the right to do what I wanted to do, to say what I wanted to say, and to act any way I wanted to act, and no one would look at me and judge me as a hypocrite.

I was in effect doing something that I had done for my entire life, which was live two separate lives. As a child I was the granddaughter of a pastor. Although she died when I was very young, I learned that she was not just any kind of pastor; she was quite remarkable in her time. She had a radio ministry from New Jersey all the way down to Virginia back in the 1940s and '50s. She pastored a Church in northern New Jersey for 17 years. She was not only an ordained elder and a pastor, I read some writings about her that made it evident that she was on track to become one of the first black female bishops to be consecrated, had she lived. And it just so happens, as genetics and other factors prevail, that while I look somewhat like my father, I look very much like my grandmother.

From the time I was a very small child people used to call me Little Mamie. My grandmother's name was Mary, but her nickname was Mamie. I was a little runt for many years growing up and I remember people patting me on my head and saying, "Look at Little Mamie. You're going to be just like your grandmother when you grow up. You're going to be a preacher just like she was." It didn't matter where I went, people who knew my grandmother would look at me and say the same thing again and again.

As I grew up, my mother began to come into her own place in this world. She decided to be a politician, which was her passion. Although she never held a public office, everyone in our sphere of influence knew who she was. She had been to the White House on multiple occasions and served on the platform committee at the 1980 Republican National Convention. She traveled to Paris, France, to serve as one of three United States delegates at the UNESCO World conference.

I went from being Little Mamie to being Pat Stuart's daughter. At no time was I just Karyn. I was always the granddaughter or the daughter of somebody who was considered great. There was no room for me to make a mistake that could potentially embarrass my family. No matter what I did, I had to make sure I did not do it at home. Be discreet in your indiscretions. Even a dog doesn't mess in his own backyard.

As I got older and more determined in my efforts to be defined as my own person, I became masterful at living a separate life that no one else knew about. I was still going to Church. I was still going to school. I was still doing everything that was expected of me. But then I also learned quickly how to have another life, away from home where no one knew who I was. That in itself is a whole other story for another book.

Even many years after being done with my indiscretions and my sinful past, there was no reason for me to continue living two lives. But it had become a part of who I was. I realized that while I was no longer hiding shameful and embarrassing and dishonorable things, I was hiding and devaluing and diminishing the magnificent work that God had done in my life. The One who loved me enough to send His son to die for me. The One to whom I know I owe everything that I am and everything that I have.

As I sat there before it was time to preach that Sunday morning, the reality and the magnitude of what that meant and what I had done suddenly hit home. I was sitting in front of just a handful of people whom I'd lived among and around yet who never knew who I really was. And in that moment I realized that it was time for me to begin Living Out Loud.

***********************************

# The Message

The story in John chapter 9 is powerful, and it's one of my favorites because of its simplicity. It's the story of a man who was born blind and who encountered Jesus the Christ one day. In verses 1 and 2 it says:

> ***Now as Jesus passed by, He saw a man who was blind from birth. And His disciples asked Him, saying, "Rabbi, who sinned, this man or his parents, that he was born blind?"***

The text says that Jesus was walking by and he saw a man who was born blind. When the disciples saw him the first thing that came to their mind was that somebody had to have sinned. And whenever I read this story and I see the response of the disciples, not just in this story but throughout the Bible, I equate the disciples with the pastors, elders, and leaders of our day. These are the men who were taught by Christ Himself, and charged and commissioned with spreading the gospel. These are the ones who Jesus poured His life into and trained and mentored and loved.

The first thing that came to their mind was that something must have happened in this situation—somebody had to sin. It's an interesting parallel to what we see now in the Church. Even among those of us who are leaders, it seems that we have developed a pattern. When we don't know the answers to hard questions and we don't know how to bring a person healing and deliverance and victory, the first thing we come up with—sometimes the only thing we come up with—is they must have done something wrong. They must have sinned to find themselves in the place where they are. Even though we all know and understand that there is a constant assault and attack on the people of God from the time of birth, even we who are leaders can find ourselves in a position where we're pointing a finger at other people and their sin.

In this particular story, Jesus makes it clear there is not anybody who sinned; not the man, not the parents.

> ***"Jesus answered, 'Neither this man nor his parents sinned, but that the works of God should be revealed in him'"*** *(John 9:3).*

That is such an interesting answer, because in it he seems to acknowledge that there are people who are born in certain states, with certain conditions, but that God never intended for them to stay that way. In this case, the whole purpose—the whole reason for any of it taking place in the way that it did—was to show that the power of God could be made manifest through that situation so that Jesus Christ Himself could be glorified.

Sometimes it seems as though we spend so much time trying to defend, define, and explain ourselves and our actions due to the way we were born, with certain personalities and traits. The thoughts and the mind-set we have developed about it has become a common mantra—this is just who I am. I'm not perfect, but nobody is perfect. I'm doing the best I can. And perhaps what this Scripture is telling us, among other things, is that one of the reasons we don't see more healing, more deliverance, and more freedom in our lives is because we have decided to define ourselves by something that God intended to heal us from so that He could get the glory.

***

Whenever I'm reading the Bible, I have this thing that I do where I actually visualize the scene. I kind of imagine myself there. I look around, smell the air, and feel the environment of the story. So, in the story in verse 6 it says:

> ***"When He had said these things, He spat on the ground and made clay with the saliva; and He anointed the eyes of the blind man with the clay" (John 9:6).***

I just want you to take a minute and enter this scene with me as I describe it based on what I personally see when I look around in the story. There are no paved roads. Nothing but a bunch of dirt roads. The people during this time had only one mode of transportation, which was something that involved an animal. In addition, there was no indoor plumbing of any kind. So they are all walking out there on the dirt roads together. Now you do understand that these animals are going to have to handle their business somewhere, someplace, and sometime, right? I don't believe anybody was walking around behind these animals with plastic bags and pooper scoopers. So in addition to the dirt there was also a whole bunch of other . . . stuff . . . mixed around and stirred up in that dirt.

This is just my view of this Scripture and these times. Of course, I do know that I am looking at this with twenty-first century eyes and twenty-first century emotions, but since that's all I have, that's the picture that gets painted for me. So the Scripture says in the sixth verse that Jesus spit on the ground and made clay with the spit. Let me stop right there. I can only speak for myself, but I do have just a wee tad of an OCD germ-o-phobe inside of me. And to be quite honest, I don't necessarily like even drinking from a water fountain behind other people. So can you imagine a concoction made up of this nasty, dusty ground and somebody's spit being mixed together into a mud pie that someone then proceeds to smear over your eyes? Lord, help!

There are several other instances in the Scriptures where Jesus healed people by various means, and I have often wondered why it was that Jesus decided to select this method in order to bring about this young man's deliverance. There are plenty of stories of Jesus laying his hands on people and even speaking to people without ever even touching them at all and the people still got healed. I can't imagine why in this instance he would choose this method in order to bring about this man's healing. Then the question came to my mind, could it be possible that some of us don't find healing and deliverance and freedom because we are not willing to allow God to demonstrate his power in our lives in the manner in which he chooses?

So, after Jesus anoints the man's eyes with the clay, he tells him to go and wash in the pool of Siloam. I'm not really sure how far the pool of Siloam was from where the man was with Jesus. But I'm wondering how exactly the man knew how to get to that particular pool. If I put myself in this story and some guy comes up to me and spits on the ground and makes some nasty mud pie and puts it on my eyes, I feel like I might be inclined to find the nearest water or even my shirt—or somebody else's shirt—or something, and get that nasty mess off my eyes. I cannot imagine being willing or even concerned about getting to a certain body of water. But in verse 7 it says:

*"So he went and washed, and came back seeing" (John 9:7).*

He went his way to that particular pool, he washed, and he came away seeing. It's interesting to note that he was willing to do exactly and only what Jesus said. I know this is not a book about healing and freedom and deliverance, but the story most certainly is, and it makes me wonder. Could it be possible that some of us can't find healing and freedom and deliverance because we are not willing to obey what God tells us to do in order to be free? I can't imagine how this blind man, who has been blind for his entire life, could get to this one specific and particular pool without getting somebody else's help. Could it be possible that some of us can't find healing and freedom and deliverance because we're not willing to allow someone else to walk with us so that we can get to the place where we will ultimately become free?

Anyway, after this situation took place, this miracle, everybody in the town was aware of what happened. The man had been blind his entire life and as a result, was a beggar. When they saw that this man who had always been blind could see, they started talking among themselves.

> ***"Therefore the neighbors and those who previously had seen that he was blind said, 'Is not this he who sat and begged?' Some said, 'This is he.' Others said, 'He is like him.' He said, 'I am he'" (John 9:8-9).***

You know how people are talking about you like you're not there and you're standing right in front of them? That's what these people were doing.

> ***"Therefore they said to him, 'How were your eyes opened?'" (John 9:10).***

When I read this story, the neighbors and people in the neighborhood represent the people in the world. These people were not saved. These people were not in the Church. They grew up around this man and they had seen and known him his entire life. They knew that the man was blind. He answered their question in verse 11:

> *"He answered and said, 'A Man called Jesus made clay and anointed my eyes and said to me, "Go to the pool of Siloam and wash." So I went and washed, and I received sight'" (John 9:11).*

This is a simple yet powerful testimony and example of this man being willing to live his life Out Loud. He was in the presence of people who had known Him his entire life, people who clearly did not know who Jesus was. He could have very easily decided that he did not want to embarrass himself and talk about his encounter with the Lord. He could have easily decided that he did not want to stand out, did not want to draw attention to himself. He could have easily made up any other lie; but instead, he decided to Live Out Loud.

All of this happened on the Sabbath day. And it seems clear from the text that this miraculous healing had gathered and stirred a great deal of attention. After he explained to the people in the neighborhood about his encounter with the Lord, the next thing you know, they brought him to the Pharisees so they could have a discussion.

> *"They brought him who formerly was blind to the Pharisees. Now it was a Sabbath when Jesus made the clay and opened his eyes. Then the Pharisees also asked him again how he had received his sight. He said to them, 'He put clay on my eyes, and I washed, and I see.' Therefore some of the Pharisees said, 'This Man is not from God,*

*because He does not keep the Sabbath.' Others said, 'How can a man who is a sinner do such signs?' And there was a division among them" (John 9:13-16).*

Conventional teaching declares that the Pharisees were the religious leaders of the day. In most instances, when people make a correlation between the Pharisees of Jesus' day and people in our day, the correlation is that they are the same as our pastors, elders, and leaders. But when I read this text, the Pharisees in this story seem to me like church people. Even though the Bible calls them religious leaders, I can never equate them with pastors, elders, and leaders of our day because if you are a pastor, elder, or leader, there should not be anything religious about you. The Pharisees clearly knew the word, but they did not know the Lord. If you have been called as a disciple by Christ, then there is no way that you could be religious at all because there is nothing religious about Christ. Spiritual, yes, but religious, absolutely not.

In my mind, religious leaders of that day could not be what God intended as the pastors, elders, and leaders through whom he would build his Church. In my mind, the only thing these Pharisees could be is church people. Some would say this is a question of semantics, and quite possibly it is so. But the way I see it, the church people were offended that this man who was born blind and was reduced to begging for his entire life was now free. They could not celebrate, appreciate, or be happy in any way to see this man experience freedom because they did not appreciate the way and the timing of when it was done. If that does not sound like church people, I don't know what does.

The Scripture says that they asked him questions about what happened. They were convinced there was no way he could be of God because even though he allegedly performed a miracle, there was no man who is of God who would've ever thought about performing a miracle on the Sabbath day. In fact, they decided he had to be a sinner. Now with any grumbling in a mixed multitude of a Church crowd, you always have people with some sense who can listen to what people are talking about and see it for what it really is.

While half of the Pharisees said there was no way this man was of God, the other half of them said a sinner wouldn't be able to perform miracles like this. They were all carrying on in front of the man who was healed and they asked him again what he could tell them about this man who'd opened his eyes? The blind man thought maybe Jesus was a prophet. But they just could not accept and believe it. By now some of them were probably convinced this man had never been blind it all, so they decided to go get the parents. And here is what the parents say in verse 19:

> ***"And they asked them, saying, 'Is this your son, who you say was born blind? How then does he now see?' His parents answered them and said, 'We know that this is our son, and that he was born blind; but by what means he now sees we do not know, or who opened his eyes we do not know. He is of age; ask him. He will speak for himself'" (John 9:19-21).***

In the face of controversy and in the face of challenge and at the time to take a stand, his parents decided to lie. Can you imagine what this must have been like for this man to be questioned about a miracle that transformed his life? Having lived his entire life in total darkness and now after meeting one man who stopped and had compassion for him, for the first time ever he could see. As a result of this miracle, which anyone in their right mind would be thrilled and excited to see, he was going through an interrogation. Not a celebration; a question-and-answer period about what happened, how it happened, and who did it. And he was standing out there all by himself. When his parents were called to explain their side of the story, instead of them standing up and speaking the truth—instead of them supporting and having their own son's back while they celebrated with him and saw his life changed—they decided to lie. I know they lied because verse 22 says that his parents answered in the way they did because they were afraid of the Jews.

> ***"His parents said these things because they feared the Jews, for the Jews had agreed already that if anyone confessed that He was Christ, he would be put out of the synagogue. Therefore his parents said, 'He is of age; ask him'" (John 9:22-23).***

The parents were concerned about being put out of the Church, about losing their position, about what it was going to cost them, so they decided it was easier for them to leave their son out there by himself. They decided to lie.

Just like I had done for years in my own life, they decided that it was easier, more convenient, and less costly for them to simply not tell the truth about what God had done. Because the truth is that now, just like then, if you make a decision to Live Out Loud and to name the name of Christ in this life, it's going to cost you something.

It dawned on me recently that spiritual and religious persecution looks entirely different in Western cultures in the twenty-first century, if you can even call it that. For the most part we are not being imprisoned, we are not being beaten, we are not suffering violence because of being a Christian and talking about what God has done or maintaining the standard of Christ in the earth. That's not what it looks like for us in this day and age. But we live in a time when anyone can publicly talk about the "Spirit" because you do know there are a lot of spirits out there, right? You can talk about the "Source." You can talk about the "Universe." You can talk about the "Light." You can talk about the "Power." You can talk about the "Energy." You can even talk about the devil. And no one will have a problem with it. Perhaps *no one* is a little bit strong; I'll just say it has become socially acceptable for people to discuss all of these things with freedom and without assault and attack.

But if you dare to simply name the name of Jesus Christ, you can probably expect a target to be printed on your back and you can probably expect hordes of assaults or accusations, just because you believe what you believe and what you believe happens to be Jesus Christ. People can believe whatever they choose to believe, but something about acknowledging the Lord Jesus Christ will instantly make you a target of attack. Many people will say that is because some of the most mean, nasty, and hateful hypocrites are in the Church. And without question, that is indeed true. In fact, I don't know of many church people who would deny that sad truth. But one could also say that some of the most mean, nasty, and hateful hypocrites are ***not*** in the Church, and so that reason alone, is not the reason for all of the judgment against people because they choose to be Christian.

Some would say Christians are the most judgmental and intolerant people around, people who cannot accept other people if they believe anything other than what they believe. And when you consider that even within the Church we have groups of people who can't even accept other groups of people because they don't believe like we believe, there is also a certain truth to those words. Those truths, however, should not ever cause any of us to fail to share the truth of what we know about Jesus Christ. No matter what our doctrine is, the truth is not our perception of what the Bible does and does not say. The truth is the reality of what Jesus Christ has done in our lives. We are living in an age when it is becoming increasingly difficult for Christians to defend their faith. The reasons are multiple and varied, but I submit to you that it is not as hard to make a stand as we think. Not hard, but it will be costly. The question for us becomes, are we willing to pay the price to Live Out Loud?

***

In the story, after the man had been questioned and the church people decided that they needed to bring in the parents, the parents decided it was easier and more convenient for them to lie. Then, in verse 23, they say something that is kind of funny to me, but it's really not funny at all. Remember in verse 22 they said we know this is our son and we know that he was born blind but we don't know what happened that he can now see? Then they basically said in verse 23 he is grown, you need to go ask him. They didn't say it exactly that way but that was pretty much it. That just cracks me up.

Anyway, they went back to the man one more time. Now keep in mind these people are religious, so they are convinced that what they are doing is exposing this Jesus, who they know was a sinner, and they are convinced that if they do that, they're going to glorify God. Please remember these are the same Pharisees who were later convinced they had to do away with that sinner called Jesus, and they were the ones who led him to the cross to be crucified. But that's a whole other story.

So when they called the man again in verse 24, they said, just glorify God and tell the truth; we know that this man Jesus is a sinner. And then the man who had been blind says something that I absolutely love. This is my favorite part of this whole story and it's in verse 25.

*"Whether He is a sinner or not I do not know. One thing I know: that though I was blind, now I see" (John 9:24).*

Simple, powerful, truth. He said I don't know anything about what you are saying. I can't answer the questions the way you want me to answer because I don't really know if what you are saying is right or whether it's wrong. All I know is I met a man, he put clay on my eyes, he told me to go wash. I went, I washed, and now I see.

In this present day it seems that it has become increasingly difficult to defend our faith. I recently heard a message by Dr. Rita Twiggs on Irrefutable Proof. It was the first time I had ever heard her speak, and it was a message that transformed my life. She spoke about all of the different religions that currently exist in our world today. When you compare Christianity to all of the other major religions of our time, Christianity is among the youngest of all of them. When you look at them side by side, they all have very similar points. When you say things like that to a Christian they get nervous, but it is still the truth. The fact is that all of the major religions have a central figure who is the representation of God. According to doctrine, that person is very wise, and that person spoke very similar truths as the God figure in every other religion. Things like, be good to people, sow good seeds, do no harm to others—basically instructing people to live what we would call decent lives.

The religions that have the central figure acknowledge that their central figure once physically lived on the earth. They acknowledge that their central figure died. The only really major difference that Christianity has that none of the others do is that when our central figure died, who is Christ, He didn't stay in the grave. He got up. And because our central figure got up—because he rose from the grave, because he ascended into heaven—that is the reason that we believe we have victorious life. But if you take that part of the story out, which of course is the most important part of the story, then Christianity looks very much like a lot of other religions.

When people are out there talking about their Gods, it is very easy for some to get confused. Everyone is calling their central figure God and they use words like we use—they talk about spirit and grace and blessing, and they say, "I believe in God." They are decent people; they are not hating or being horribly rude, mean, nasty, disrespectful people. They are trying to be kind and trying to be good and trying to be gracious—all attributes that we consider important.

It is easy to get confused when you try to intellectually explain to someone how a person could die and be raised from the dead and be seated in heaven and yet still live within me. It's hard because the story is so wild and totally out there that there is no way you can understand it intellectually. In a culture where we worship and idolize intellect the way we do, it is challenging to speak about something that even the Apostle Paul called foolishness.

That's one of the reasons I love this story so much, because it is a picture of what we as Christians deal with today. Sometimes it's harder to Live Out Loud in the Church than it is in the world. Even when you try to make a stand to live your truth and walk in what God is calling you to do, the people in the Church can treat you worse than the people in the world. But no matter what anybody thinks about it, the one thing that no one can refute is what God has done in your life.

This man who was blind was very simple in telling his story. In the simplicity of sharing his own story there was such power, because he had nothing to stand on except his own experience. When faced with questions and arguments that he simply could not answer, he did not try to make something up so he would sound spiritual. He did not become argumentative or defensive because he could not answer them. He did not repeat something that he heard somebody else say and try to pretend like he knew what he was talking about. All he said was what he knew for sure. He said, all I know is, I once was blind and now I see. At the end of the day, it did not matter if they believed it or did not believe it. If they agreed or disagreed. If they liked it or did not like it. At the end of the day, his truth could not be denied, and the same is true for us.

It does not matter what anyone else thinks about it, our truth—the reality of what God has done in our own lives—cannot be denied. It is no wonder there is such a challenge and assault against Christians sharing the simple truth of their testimony. Even in the Church we have come to devalue and undervalue the power of our testimony. There used to be a time when almost every Church service began with people sharing what the Lord had done in their lives. For some reason, even in the Church, we have come to a point where we think it is not important to share our testimonies anymore. It is a curious position for us to take, especially when the word is clear that says we overcome the enemy by the blood of the lamb and the word of our testimony (***Revelation 12:11***).

I believe part of that challenge comes from the fact that in order to tell you what God has done in my life, I have to share my own deficiency, some area where I am lacking. I have to share some of the decisions that I have made and the consequences that followed. I have to let you see and know the imperfections of my life so you can understand what God did to change them. I believe that is a big part of why we don't freely talk about what God has done in our lives; the fear and shame about the journeys of our past, even those areas where God has set us free.

If you think about it, our testimonies really have nothing to do with our worthiness. In fact, when we testify and share our story, it is really not about us at all. It is the story of the greatness of God. We are hiding from a world that desperately needs to hear our voice.

People are all around us who don't even believe that God still does miracles today. When we come out of hiding, we become the living epistles that demonstrate the truth of who God is.

There are few things that we can do or share that are more powerful than telling what great things the Lord has done in our lives. And what is the big deal if people get uncomfortable and don't want to hear what we have to say? What exactly is the problem, when we have to sit and listen to them talking all day, every day, about how bad things are, how out of control this world is, how the government is falling apart, and how you can't trust anybody at any time for anything? Why is it okay for me to have to listen to their words, which have absolutely no life? And if I do, what is the problem for other people to have to listen to the story of my life and what God has done for me?

I believe another of the reasons we don't share is because just like the parents of the man in the story, we realize that if we begin to live our lives Out Loud and share the reality of our truth, it is very likely going to cost us something. In some instances, it is possible that we have decided that we are simply not willing to pay the price. I cannot imagine anyone actually saying those words out of their mouth, but our inward choices dictate our outward actions.

When it comes to sharing the truth of who God is, we can only walk in the light that has been revealed to us as of this day. We can only talk about what we know about Him today. We are all being changed from glory to glory as we walk out our relationship with God. (*2 Corinthians 3:18*). And we are all gaining deeper and deeper knowledge of Him as we continue on this journey. If we continue to pursue Him and seek His face, He will continue to reveal to us greater and deeper truths.

Today, I am not responsible for those greater and deeper truths. What I am responsible for is the truth that has been revealed in me.

Sometimes I wonder if the reason we as Christians are so quiet and timid and shy and without power is because we know in our hearts that, although we call ourselves Christians, and we name the name of Christ when we are among one another, the fact is we really don't know Him at all. We've been going through the motions; but could it be possible that the reason we don't share is because we know that we don't live what we preach? We have come to a point where we live such lives of compromise that we no longer feel we have the power of effective witness.

Jesus said in Acts 1:8 that the Holy Spirit would give power to be a witness throughout the entire earth. But we can't even agree on what it means to be filled with the Spirit, and we don't even agree whether we want to be or not! So we live lives that cause our hearts to condemn us and keep us silent in a world that is crying out for our voice, waiting for those who have seen God and testify that He does in fact exist and He is in fact real. Not the voice of our doctrine, not the voice of our individual beliefs about what His word says or even means, but the voice of the truth, which is Jesus Christ. If we are going to survive in these times it's time for us to rise up and begin to speak our truth and make a commitment to radical obedience to the One who saved and ransomed our lives. Radical obedience equals Living Out Loud.

# Radical Obedience

Radical obedience seems like a foreign concept in our world. If you take a look at parents interacting with their children in public the next time you go to the grocery store it is quite clear that we place little value on obedience. We now believe that children should have a voice and they should have a right to choose to agree and comply with what feels right to them. Those children will become adults who have no interest in submitting to authority. We have become a people who feel that we should be bound by no rules or laws except those that make sense or are convenient for us. And this logic makes perfect sense to us.

If I were to honestly evaluate my current state of obedience, I would have to say it is based on convenience and what I am actually willing to give up or lose. It so often seems that to radically obey God, I have to give up something, I have to lose something, I have to let something die. And honestly, if I lay it open bare, that's where this thing becomes a problem. I love God. I want to serve Him. I want to please Him. But I also want peace, comfort, prosperity, and rest. I want what I want. I want what I feel will make me happy.

I do not want to do anything that will cause me distress, discomfort, or loss of any kind. That is just my truth. I am a product of my culture. I feel that I have certain rights to a certain kind of life, and that life is one of MY choosing. I feel that there is nothing I shouldn't be able or allowed to do or choose. I believe in the boundaries of the law for the most part, even though I break the law willingly and knowingly every single time I get behind the wheel of my car. I mean, I understand that the law states that each road has an upper limit of speed that should not be passed but really, if I am not reckless or doing anything to hurt anyone, and if I only go a certain number above what the law says, what exactly is such a big deal about that? I live in a world where anything that limits me is subject to my agreement or consent—if I agree and I want to, then I will do it. If not, I will not. I am over the age of 21, so really I can choose to do or not do whatever I wish. I understand that all actions are accompanied by consequences, and I am not afraid of consequence. Each time I decide to speed, I am also willing to pay a speeding ticket should I get caught—a small price to pay in order to do whatever I want.

We see no connection between this thinking and attitude and the spiraling decline of our culture. The time and generation that I live in has championed my right to be whoever I want to be—to shape and frame the world I live in based on what seems best to me—to live the life that makes me happy. I *deserve* this. I am encouraged to celebrate all that I am, both good and bad, and love myself just the way I am. I am told to take care of myself first so I will have enough energy and strength to care for others. All of this makes perfect sense to me. The theology of my culture and world puts me and my wants and my needs front and center in the first position in my life—and everything else follows, including God.

And even when we hear the Gospel preached, we rarely if ever hear anything about what we give in exchange for a life following Christ. In fact, the One many sign up for is the One who will save them from death and hell and all the other unpleasant stuff that makes life uncomfortable. And let's face it, who wouldn't want to make a deal with some big, powerful God who had the ability to do all that cool stuff? That message fits very nicely in the confines of our culture and world.

Sadly, there are many who at no time really consider the whole concept of Jesus as Lord and what that actually means. And so, since we signed up for a relationship with this great, big, amazing God who could do anything for us, then anything that may be asked of me that would seem like I would have to lose or get the short end of the stick, could not possibly be God. That is not who He is in my life. He is the God who makes all things good and new. He is the God who meets all of my needs. He is the God who answers all of my prayers. Basically, He is the God who makes my life better, and anything that may cause me any discomfort or displeasure on any level cannot possibly be God. Anything or anyone who asks of me something that will not make me happy cannot be of God because this whole thing is supposed to be about the better (however I view that) life I am supposed to have.

Jesus as Savior I've got all day, but Jesus as Lord is something entirely different. What does that even mean? Is he not Savior of the world? Of course he is; but Philippians 2:10-11 says every knee shall bow and every tongue confess Jesus Christ is LORD. We can almost tolerate Him as Savior in a world that focuses everything on me, but to see Him, acknowledge Him, submit to Him as Lord, that's a whole other thing. Because the word *Lord* means Master, Owner, Possessor. When you OWN something, you have full, total, complete control over that thing. The idea of that brings this whole Christianity thing into a different light. That means I really am NOT in control of my destiny, my happiness, my well-being. At the very most I can make a choice to count it all joy. But this Lord thing means that someone else gets to tell me what I can and cannot do. Someone else gets to decide where I will and will not go. And if someone OWNS me, then it doesn't matter if I like it or don't like it, agree or disagree, want to or don't want to. My life is not my own and I do not get a vote. Surely that is not what this means!!! Surely, it is.

Radical obedience demands my unwavering, non-negotiable willingness to do whatever God asks, whenever he asks, however he asks. And as extreme as this concept may seem, in reality it is very much Christianity 101. Somehow, at some point, we in the Church began to water down the gospel and sell it in a more palatable form. We no longer teach and preach that you need to lay down your life to take on his.

We have become a people who have attempted to ADD His life to ours instead of EXCHANGE our life for His. What we are left with is an afflicted, hybrid, powerless religion that is void of Spirit and of Life and of power. And so when we pray, we rarely see things happen and in truth, we often don't bother to even pray much at all. Since we see so little fruit and results for our Christian activities, we see little reason to devote our hearts to the pursuit of His purpose. We are content to come to Church and even work in the Church, but when it comes to forsaking all to follow Him, most of us never signed up for that. We don't mind the pursuit of spiritual activities, we just want to do it on our own terms, in a manner that is convenient for us and still allows us to have a personal life that we can actually enjoy.

There is no room for radical obedience to what God says because if the truth be told, the average Christian does not even know what it means to hear God's voice and hear it consistently. So if we can't even consistently hear God's voice, how is it possible for us to radically obey Him?

Some of us are not even sure we believe God still speaks to people today. We also believe that there are just certain things that God would never ask us to do and that we should not be expected to do. We have developed the notion that our personal life and our spiritual life are two different things. We should not have to be focused on Church, spiritual, or religious things all the time. "God would never ask me to do that." That is actually a true statement. God is not interested in all the churchy religious things that we spend our time doing. What He IS interested in and does require is that at all times, in all things, our focus and our eyes are only on Him. He wants us to see Him in every situation and circumstance. He wants us to be so close to Him that we not only hear His voice, but the voice of a stranger we would not follow. He wants us to have one life where He is all in all.

Once we submit to this kind of life, radical obedience is a natural byproduct, as is Living Out Loud. There is no God life and my life. My life is hidden with Christ in God and whatever He requires is what I choose to do.

# The End of this Story

This entire book is really just a story. It is the story of one segment of my life, albeit an impactful one, and one simple man with one simple story full of power. There are specific moments in our lives—defining moments that separate the spectacular from the mundane, like specific turns in the road that lead you to a new place or in a different direction. The moment of decision is not the physical arrival at the next destination but at the same time it is. That point of decision is the guarantee of what you have set your heart to pursue or to do. I call it being settled on the question. It is the point where you eliminate all other options concerning a certain thing—when you decide there will be no turning back. And so there is no end to this story except that of a commitment to radical obedience.

I believe there is a clarion call sounding throughout the earth, asking the question of us who believe. Are you ready to lay down your life in exchange for His? To allow Him to heal you of the things that have held you back and held you down? To not just allow Him to do that, but allow Him to do it His way? Are we willing to follow His instructions and Live our lives Out Loud with radical obedience and boldness? Are we ready to join together with other believers and allow them to walk with us and help us and guide us and then do the same for them? And are we ready to glorify God no matter what it costs us? There is no question that a radical life in Christ is costly. And it is probably harder if you are not a person who is in some kind of full-time ministry or service. When you are out among people who are not talking like you, who don't believe like you, and in many cases do not even care about what you know or believe—that's when the test will come.

I can say that in most ways I have considered myself to be obedient to God, but there has always been that open door—that way out if the thing being asked of me was really not something I wanted to do or even felt like I could do. As much as I liked to say that no matter what the Lord asks of me I will do it, the truth is, I have always picked the things I have chosen to say yes to. Sometimes saying yes was going to cost me more than I was willing to pay. There has never been a question about God's heart concerning obedience. There are a ton of Scriptures concerning it. These two passages in 1 Samuel immediately come to mind:

> *1 Samuel 15:22*
> ***"So Samuel said: 'Has the Lord as great delight in burnt offerings and sacrifices, As in obeying the voice of the Lord? Behold, to obey is better than sacrifice, And to heed than the fat of rams.'"***
>
> *1 Samuel 12:14-15*
> ***"If you fear the Lord and serve Him and obey His voice, and do not rebel against the commandment of the Lord, then both you and the king who reigns over you will continue following the Lord your God. However, if you do not obey the voice of the Lord, but rebel against the commandment of the Lord, then the hand of the Lord will be against you, as it was against your fathers."***

So I could never say that I did not understand God's heart, but there were always so many other problems with the concept of complete, radical, total obedience.

What if I am wrong? What if I thought I heard the Lord say something but it wasn't Him or what if I misunderstood exactly what it was He was asking me to do? What if I didn't sense His timing right? I know that Jesus said His sheep know His voice, and I know there have definitely been times when I was pretty sure I heard God speak. But what if this thing I think I am hearing is not even God at all? Then in my effort to be obedient, what kind of damage could I be causing, to myself or to others, with some crazy idea, or word, or notion? And even though I know the Scripture, is that still really true? DO people actually still hear the voice of God? How do you know when you have heard it, and can something like that actually be taught?

# Hearing God's Voice

I met a guy over 15 years ago up in Canada named Mark Virkler. I was in a time of separation with God, 30 days away from home, seeking Him to determine how or if I would move forward in life in the areas I believed he was calling me to. I never actually knew what I was supposed to do, but I knew that I was supposed to do something for God. I knew that I had an oratory gift, so preaching always came very naturally and organically for me. I started preaching when I was 15 years old, even though when I started preaching I was not even saved (also a story for a whole other book). Back then—and still today in some circles—if you are a woman with some type of call on your life, the thought is that you are an evangelist, or at least that is what your title must be. The other more progressive idea is that you might possibly even be called a pastor. The evangelist thing always bothered me because I could never understand how being a woman just automatically made me an evangelist, even though I saw absolutely no scriptural support for the concept or idea. And I also could not settle on the idea that just because I preached that meant I was supposed to be a pastor. But back then, that was pretty much all anyone talked about in my circles so I never felt like I found my right "suit" in ministry—I just knew I had some kind of call, and I knew I could preach with relative ease.

I knew inside that I was supposed to do something for God, with God, but I had no real firm conviction of what that thing should be and I never felt like I should have to drive it or build it like one does seemed to me that if I was called to do something, I should now it with some measure of confidence and just walk in ... years of doing whatever it was I was doing, I reached somewhat of a crisis of faith. I needed to know with some degree of certainty what it was that God wanted me to do with my life and in particular, if that something included ministry (also another story for a whole other book).

It was during this time of searching that I found myself in Canada at a ministry where Mark Virkler was one of the teachers. During his week of teaching, his subject was Communion with God. The organizers had made this bold and startling promise; at the end of this week, you WILL hear the voice of God. I was immediately annoyed and offended because I felt like I was being lied to. How can you "teach" someone to hear God's voice? Either you do or you don't. And to make a declarative statement like that just offended me.

Fast forward 15 years and I will make my own bold, declarative statement—you can be taught to hear the voice of God and I am living proof. If you are interested in learning I will recommend two books by this same guy who taught me. They are *4 Keys to Hearing God's Voice* and *Dialogue with God.* They are both phenomenal books that if studied and applied will absolutely transform your life.

# Obey My Voice

*Jeremiah 7:22-23*
*"For I did not speak to your fathers, or command them in the day that I brought them out of the land of Egypt, concerning burnt offerings or sacrifices. But this is what I commanded them saying, 'Obey my voice, and I will be your God, and you shall be my people. And walk in all the ways that I have commanded you, that it may be well with you.'"*

*Genesis 3:4-6 (NLT)*
*"'You won't die!' the serpent replied to the woman. 'God knows that your eyes will be opened as soon as you eat it, and you will be like God, knowing both good and evil.' The woman was convinced. She saw that the tree was beautiful and its fruit looked delicious, and she wanted the wisdom it would give her. So she took some of the fruit and ate it. Then she gave some to her husband, who was with her, and he ate it, too."*

If you read the text in Genesis carefully, it speaks of the fall of man, and the whole thing is centered on one thing; you do not have to listen to or obey God's voice. You can be like God and know whatever you want to know yourself if you just eat of this tree.

Here is this man, Adam, and he has the amazing privilege of

walking with God and talking to Him in the garden. Can you imagine physically walking in this place of paradise with the very one who created you? There is no boundary, no separation, nothing between you and the one who made you. Every time I think about it, it just blows my mind.

So anyway, the whole temptation was based on an offer that would allow the man to substitute or exchange that experience for the ability to know whatever he wanted to know without ever having to ask God. To be "like" God without having to interact "with" God. When you look at it in that context, it seems like the most ludicrous thought and idea ever. But that was the foundation of the temptation . . . that, and the fact that God clearly lied when He said they would die.

Even all these years later, we are still tricked by that same temptation constantly every single day. We have become so fully convinced that we each have a perfectly adequate mind of our own and we can use it to make whatever decisions we think are best, and none of that requires us to consult with God or anyone else. We are so perfectly self-centered and self-conscious that the idea of looking to God for direction in every area of our lives seems completely ridiculous. I have a mind and I am entirely capable of using it.

Since this has been our position, it is really not even important to us to hear God's voice at all unless we have a situation that we cannot seem to figure out without Him. We have relegated the voice of God to the role of a reference tool to be consulted only when we are not able to work it out or figure it out for ourselves. And since His voice is so foreign to us and ultimately so unimportant, obeying it really cannot be that high on the list of our priorities. Living by and obeying a set of rules is something we are comfortable with . . . except when it comes to the Bible. We all agree that it is simply not even possible to obey every single rule in the Bible. So what does obeying God's voice really mean? It's simple, really. Follow the voice and leading of the Spirit of God that dwells within you. If you abide in me and I in you . . . (John 15:4). That is not just memorizing Scripture but honoring the present, living word of the Lord that lives in you, and yielding to and obeying His voice in your life. So obedience ***is not*** about do this or don't do that. Obedience ***is*** about doing or not doing, saying or not saying, going or not going, based on what the indwelling Spirit of God speaks to you every moment of every day. Radical obedience is about doing that no matter how it looks, how you feel about it, or what other people say about it. Radical—without exception. Not as long as I think it is fair. Radical—without exception. Not as long as it does not cost me too much. Radical—without exception. Not as long as it will not make me look stupid. Radical—without exception. Not as long as it is convenient for me. Radical—without exception. Not as long as it makes sense to me. Radical—without exception.

# Beyond the Comfort Zone

We have become masterful at following the safe and unobstructed path. Even some of our bold steps and moves have been made with a Plan B in mind. But I'm talking about going way far out in the Abraham zone. That is where this road is headed. The court of public opinion will be the worst enemy and among the biggest challenges, and the opinions of those in the Church will be far worse than those without. This kind of life will challenge and disturb the most religious of people and they will rail against you, just like they did Jesus. Remember, it was not the heathens who killed Jesus, it was the church people. So when you make this decision, the heat will be on. Attacks, assaults, and insults will be plentiful and common. At times you may feel like a total and complete fool, and those around you will tell you that is exactly what you are. They will challenge your faith, your knowledge of God, and even your sanity. They will declare that "God would never ask you to do that" . . . because they know they would never do it.

God is calling us to go beyond our comfort and our convenience. He is calling us to a life without a net. He is calling us to a life where He is the only thing that will keep us safe. The One that gives us direction. The One that gives us counsel. I'm not saying that there should not be confirmation. Out of the mouth of two or three witnesses let every word be established (2 Corinthians 13:1). Nor am I saying there should not be accountability. In the multitude of counselors there is safety (Proverbs 11:14 and 26:4). What I am saying is that our lives will not be governed or guided by our own agenda or by anyone else's.

Just like the pillar of cloud by day and the pillar of fire by night, God intends to give His direction, which we diligently seek as if our very lives depend on it. This sounds so extreme and so radical because it is. In a culture that encourages us to put ourselves first, God is calling us to a counterculture that requires us to put Him first, not in word but in deed. What does that mean? What does that look like? That looks like potentially enduring things that we don't feel we should have to endure. That means being willing to look and be called foolish. That means doing something that He asks even if we are afraid that we might do it wrong. That means trusting Him on an entirely different level, not just saying or singing the words "I trust you, Lord," but in deed. This is living a life that rises up to our words. When He says speak, we speak. When He says stand, we stand. When we see injustice and things that are not of God and He moves us and instructs us to speak, we no longer remain silent but speak His truth in love.

He is not calling us to be some kind of wild crusaders running around the earth trying to correct every injustice we see. But He is calling us to come out of the shadows, to be seen and known for who we really are, which is a showcase of His glory and a carrier of His spirit in the earth. It could be something as simple as sitting next to someone, smiling at someone, or actually speaking a word in some particular place at some time. There is no formula, and it will look as different and unique as we are as individuals who are strategically and divinely sent to fulfill His purpose. He is calling us to cultivate a life with Him in the secret place and live that life in the presence of others. Not just in Church among those who are our own, but to live that life in the world around us. It's fine to come to Church and speak a word of encouragement and be spiritual around other church people, but we are called to be salt and light to the *world.*

> *Matthew 5:13-16*
> ***"You are the salt of the earth; but if the salt loses its flavor, how shall it be seasoned? It is then good for nothing but to be thrown out and trampled underfoot by men. You are the light of the world. A city that is set on a hill cannot be hidden. Nor do they light a lamp and put it under a basket, but on a lampstand, and it gives light to all who are in the house. Let your light so shine before men, that they may see your good works and glorify your Father in heaven."***

It's important to note that God's instruction to us may not always seem to make sense. But our obedience to the voice of God cannot be contingent upon whether or not it makes sense to us.

I cannot imagine it made sense to Abraham to just leave home with everything he owned and trust that God would show him the way as he went, but he obeyed.

> *Gen 12:1-4*
> ***"Now the Lord had said to Abram: 'Get out of your country, From your family And from your father's house, To a land that I will show you. I will make you a great nation; I will bless you And make your name great; And you shall be a blessing. I will bless those who bless you, And I will curse him who curses you; And in you all the families of the earth shall be blessed.' So Abram departed as the Lord had spoken to him."***

I cannot imagine it made sense to Abraham when God told him

to sacrifice Isaac after he waited 25 years just for the child to be born, but he obeyed.

> *Genesis 22:1-3*
> *"Now it came to pass after these things that God tested Abraham, and said to him, 'Abraham!' And he said, 'Here I am.' Then He said, 'Take now your son, your only son Isaac, whom you love, and go to the land of Moriah, and offer him there as a burnt offering on one of the mountains of which I shall tell you.' So Abraham rose early in the morning and saddled his donkey, and took two of his young men with him, and Isaac his son."*

I cannot imagine it made sense to Joshua when he went out to fight the battle at Jericho that the plan was just to march around the city once a day for seven days. What kind of battle plan is that? But he obeyed.

> *Joshua 6:4-5 (NLT)*
> *"Seven priests will walk ahead of the Ark, each carrying a ram's horn. On the seventh day you are to march around the town seven times, with the priests blowing the horns. When you hear the priests give one long blast on the rams' horns, have all the people shout as loud as they can. Then the walls of the town will collapse, and the people can charge straight into the town."*

It could not have made sense to Ananias for God to tell him to go and find a man who had tortured and harassed Christians with authority from the chief priests, and lay hands on him so he could receive his sight. But he obeyed.

*Acts 9:10-17*
*"Now there was a certain disciple at Damascus named Ananias; and to him the Lord said in a vision, 'Ananias.' And he said, 'Here I am, Lord.' So the Lord said to him, 'Arise and go to the street called Straight, and inquire at the house of Judas for one called Saul of Tarsus, for behold, he is praying. And in a vision he has seen a man named Ananias coming in and putting his hand on him, so that he might receive his sight.' Then Ananias answered, 'Lord, I have heard from many about this man, how much harm he has done to Your saints in Jerusalem. And here he has authority from the chief priests to bind all who call on Your name.' But the Lord said to him, 'Go, for he is a chosen vessel of Mine to bear My name before Gentiles, kings, and the children of Israel. For I will show him how many things he must suffer for My name's sake.' And Ananias went his way and entered the house; and laying his hands on him he said, 'Brother Saul, the Lord Jesus, who appeared to you on the road as you came, has sent me that you may receive your sight and be filled with the Holy Spirit.'"*

The instruction that God gives us may not always make sense, and this makes learning to recognize His voice clearly one of the most important pursuits of our lives. If obedience requires me to know exactly what God is saying to me, I have got to be able to recognize His voice. Not just for when I am in crisis or when I can't figure something out, but so that I can live a life of obedience to His will for my life every single day.

By no means am I saying this radical obedience thing is easy, or even that I meet this goal 100 percent of the time. I am even now challenged as I write these words because I recognize that my own life of surrender is not complete. It is a challenging and difficult journey. But to this life have I been called. I can only acknowledge this truth for myself, as only you can for yourself. I don't believe this was meant to be a reality for only certain Christians. Unless you own this as your truth you will never make the commitment to God to live the life you were created to live. In order to truly live our lives Out Loud, we have to be willing to obey the voice of God no matter what it costs and no matter what it takes. When we sell out to that degree and on that level, that's when all the cool and amazing stuff, the greater works that Jesus spoke of in John 14:12, begins to happen every day in our lives. I am ready to come out of hiding so God can show Himself strong in my life and in the earth. I am ready to start Living Out Loud!

Are you in???

# Epilogue

Decisions require action or else they are just talk. If by turning this page in this book you are also ready to turn the page in your life, let's take this action together. Start by praying this prayer:

Father, you know my heart and you know my story. You know why I have been hiding out and I know you are challenging me to give up my safe existence, trust you, and step into your light. I won't lie to you, this thing scares me. I really don't even fully know what this will look like or mean in my life, but I am willing to make the commitment to you today to come out of hiding, trust you with my heart and my life, and be radically obedient to you as you lead me by your Spirit from this day forward for the rest of my life. This day represents a milepost on the timeline of my life. It is the day when I am crossing the point of no return. The question is not whether I will serve you or not, but whether I will exchange my will for your will, Live my life Out Loud, and be radically obedient by the strength of your power. I am fully aware that I can do nothing in and of myself, and I surrender my heart and will to you that you may do this in and through me. And thank you, Lord, for loving me enough to allow me to be a part of what you are doing and will do to transform the world. In the name of the One who is greater than all, Jesus the Christ. Amen.

If you prayed that prayer there is one more step for you to take. I need for you to go to my website: karynstuart.com, and let me know.

What's the point of that? For some of you, this will serve as your first declaration to the world of the choice you have just made. I want to hear about it and know who you are. I want a chance to get to know the people who are fighting and serving in this revolution with me. Another reason this is important is that none of us can do this alone. In fact, the plan of God has never been for us as his people to live our lives alone. We absolutely need the prayer, love, encouragement, and support of others who are walking this path with us. I would be lying if I told you what this journey will look like for you. I have no idea what it will even look like for me. But I am sure that this bold decision you have just made will be met with resistance. I want to build a community of warriors who will build relationship with each other and leave no wounded soldier to die.

This is where all the really cool God Stuff begins!

#LivingOutLoud… the ***new*** LOL

32081339R00038

Made in the USA
San Bernardino, CA
27 March 2016